Piyaporn

# European Word Book

# English
# Spanish
# French
# German

**Brown Watson**

ENGLAND

# Contents

ISBN 978-0-7097-1913-7
First published 2011 by Brown Watson
The Old Mill, 76 Fleckney Road,
Kibworth Beauchamp,
LE8 0HG, ENGLAND

**F = French  S = Spanish  G = German**

# The Family
## La famille

### father
F le père
S el padre
G der Vater

### mother
F la mère
S la madre
G die Mutter

### grandfather
F le grand-père
S el abuelo
G der Großvater

### grandmother
F la grand-mère
S la abuela
G die Großmutter

### brother
F le frère
S el hermano
G der Bruder

### sister
F la soeur
S la hermana
G die Schwester

### aunt
F la tante
S la tía
G die Tante

### daughter
F la fille
S la hija
G die Tochter

### son
F le fils
S el hijo
G der Sohn

### uncle
F l'oncle
S el tío
G der Onkel

# Our Bodies
## Nos corps

**mouth**
- F la bouche
- S la boca
- G der Mund

**hair**
- F les cheveux
- S el cabello
- G die Haare

**eye**
- F l'œil
- S el ojo
- G das Auge

**head**
- F la tête
- S la cabeza
- G der Kopf

**nose**
- F le nez
- S la nariz
- G die Nase

**arm**
- F le bras
- S el brazo
- G der Arm

**knee**
- F le genou
- S la rodilla
- G das Knie

**back**
- F le dos
- S la espalda
- G der Rücken

**foot**
- F le pied
- S el pie
- G der Fuß

**leg**
- F la jambe
- S la pierna
- G das Bein

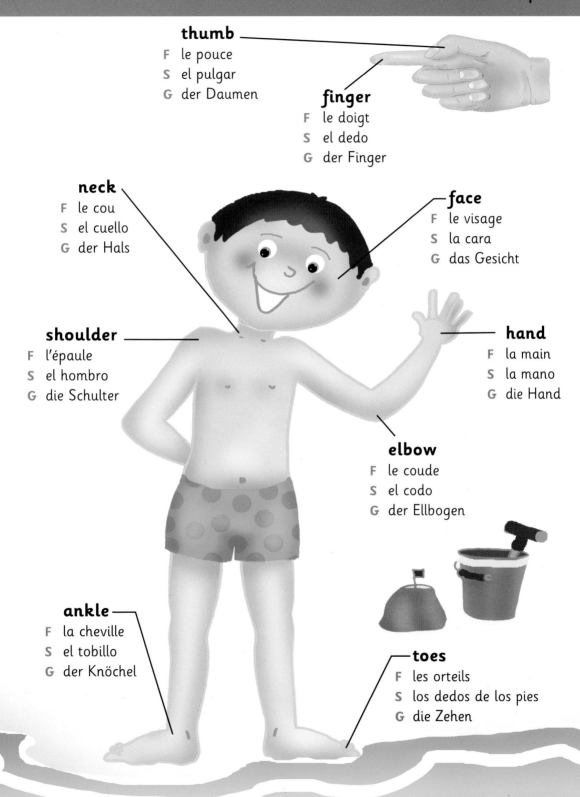

**thumb**
F   le pouce
S   el pulgar
G   der Daumen

**finger**
F   le doigt
S   el dedo
G   der Finger

**neck**
F   le cou
S   el cuello
G   der Hals

**face**
F   le visage
S   la cara
G   das Gesicht

**shoulder**
F   l'épaule
S   el hombro
G   die Schulter

**hand**
F   la main
S   la mano
G   die Hand

**elbow**
F   le coude
S   el codo
G   der Ellbogen

**ankle**
F   la cheville
S   el tobillo
G   der Knöchel

**toes**
F   les orteils
S   los dedos de los pies
G   die Zehen

# More People Words
## Plus de mots sur les gens

### family
- F la famille
- S la familia
- G die Familie

### twins
- F les jumelles
- S los mellizos
- G die Zwillinge

### woman
- F la dame
- S la mujer
- G die Frau

### girl
- F la fille
- S la niña
- G das Mädchen

### boy
- F le garçon
- S el niño
- G der Junge

### man
- F le monsieur
- S el hombre
- G der Mann

### child
- F l'enfant
- S el niño
- G das Kind

### wife
F la femme
S la esposa
G die Ehefrau

### husband
F le mari
S el esposo
G der Ehemann

### friends
F les amis
S los amigos
G die Freunde

### cousins
F les cousins/cousines
S los primos
G die Cousins

### children
F les enfants
S los niños
G die Kinder

### baby
F le bébé
S el bebé
G das Baby

# Clothes
## Les vêtements

### T-shirt
F le tee-shirt
S la camiseta
G das T-Shirt

### skirt
F la jupe
S la falda
G der Rock

### dressing gown
F la robe de chambre
S la bata
G der Morgenmantel

### socks
F les chaussettes
S las medias
G die Socken

### coat
F le manteau
S el abrigo
G der Mantel

### anorak
F l'anorak
S la chaqueta
G der Anorak

### shorts
F le short
S los pantalones cortos
G die Shorts

### cap
F la casquette
S el gorro
G die Mütze

### pyjamas
F le pyjama
S el pijamas
G der Schlafanzug

### dress
F la robe
S el vestido
G das Kleid

### cardigan
F le gilet
S el buzo
G die Strickjacke

### shirt
F la chemise
S la camisa
G das Hemd

### trousers
F le pantalon
S los pantalones
G die Hose

### hat
F le chapeau
S el sombrero
G der Hut

### gloves
F les gants
S los guantes
G die Handschuhe

### nightdress
F la chemise de nuit
S el vestido de noche
G das Nachthemd

# More Things to Wear
## Plus de choses à porter

### swimming shorts
F le maillot de bain
S el bañador
G die Badehose

### sandals
F les sandales
S las sandalias
G die Sandalen

### handbag
F le sac à main
S la cartera
G die Handtasche

### boots
F les bottes
S las botas
G die Stiefel

### shoes
F les chaussures
S los zapatos
G die Schuhe

### slippers
F les pantoufles
S las pantuflas
G die Hausschuhe

### trainers
F les baskets
S las zapatillas
G die Turnschuhe

### belt
F la ceinture
S el cinturón
G der Gürtel

**jewellery**
F les bijoux
S las joyas
G der Schmuck

**suit**
F le costume
S el traje
G der Anzug

**uniform**
F l'uniforme
S el uniforme
G die Uniform

# The Bedroom
## La chambre

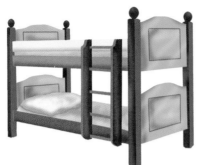

### bunk beds
F les lits superposés
S la litera
G die Etagenbetten

### wardrobe
F la garde-robe
S el ropero
G der Schrank

### pictures
F les images
S los cuadros
G die Bilder

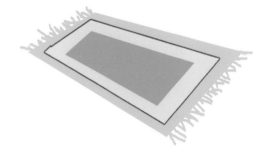

### rug
F le tapis
S la alfombra
G der Vorleger

### alarm clock
F le réveil
S el reloj alarma
G der Wecker

### lamp
F la lampe
S la lámpara
G die Lampe

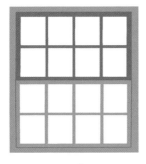

### window
F la fenêtre
S la ventana
G das Fenster

### curtains
F les rideaux
S las cortinas
G die Vorhänge

### bed
F le lit
S la cama
G das Bett

### pillow
F l'oreiller
S la almohada
G das Kissen

### cot
F le lit de bébé
S la cuna
G das Kinderbett

### chest of drawers
F la commode
S la mesa de luz
G die Kommode

# The Bathroom
## La salle de bain

### taps
F les robinets
S las canillas
G die Wasserhähne

### bath
F le bain
S la bañera
G die Badewanne

### shower
F la douche
S la ducha
G die Dusche

### toilet
F le WC
S el inodoro
G die Toilette

### wash basin
F le lavabo
S la pileta
G das Waschbecken

### towel
**F** la serviette
**S** la toalla
**G** das Handtuch

### sponge
**F** l'éponge
**S** la esponja
**G** der Schwamm

### scales
**F** la balance
**S** la balanza
**G** die Waage

### toilet paper
**F** le papier hygiénique
**S** el papel higiénico
**G** das Toilettenpapier

### potty
**F** le pot
**S** la pelela
**G** das Töpfchen

### soap
**F** le savon
**S** el jabón
**G** die Seife

### toothpaste
**F** le dentifrice
**S** la pasta de dientes
**G** die Zahnpasta

### toothbrush
**F** la brosse à dents
**S** el cepillo de dientes
**G** die Zahnbürste

# The Kitchen
## La cuisine

**kettle**
F la bouilloire
S la caldera
G der Wasserkocher

**mugs**
F les mugs
S las tazas
G die Becher

**teapot**
F la théière
S la tetera
G die Teekanne

**cupboard**
F le placard
S la alacena
G der Geschirrschrank

**microwave**
F le micro-onde
S el microondas
G die Mikrowelle

**oven**
F le four
S el horno
G der Ofen

**vacuum cleaner**
F l'aspirateur
S la aspiradora
G der Staubsauger

## washing machine
F la machine à laver
S el lavarropas
G die Waschmaschine

## sink
F l'évier
S la pileta
G das Spülbecken

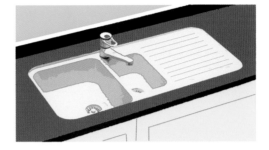

## refrigerator
F le réfrigérateur
S el refrigerador
G der Kühlschrank

## dishwasher
F le lave-vaisselle
S el lavavajillas
G die Geschirrspülmaschine

## freezer
F le congélateur
S el congelador
G der Gefrierschrank

# The Living Room
## Le salon

**door**
F  la porte
S  la puerta
G  die Tür

**television**
F  la télévision
S  la televisión
G  der Fernseher

**picture**
F  le tableau
S  la fotografía
G  das Bild

**telephone**
F  le téléphone
S  el teléfono
G  das Telefon

**flowers**
F  les fleurs
S  las flores
G  die Blumen

**magazines**
F  les magazines
S  las revistas
G  die Zeitschriften

### painting
F la peinture
S la pintura
G das Gemälde

### DVD player
F le lecteur DVD
S el reproductor de DVD
G der DVD-Spieler

### newspapers
F les journaux
S los periódicos
G die Zeitungen

### MP3 player
F le baladeur MP3
S el reproductor MP3
G der MP3-Spieler

### fireplace
F la cheminée
S el hogar
G der Kamin

### cushions
F les coussins
S los almohadones
G die Kissen

# The Dining Room
## La salle à manger

**mirror**
F le miroir
S el espejo
G der Spiegel

**plates**
F les assiettes
S los platos
G die Teller

**cup**
F la tasse
S la taza
G die Tasse

**saucer**
F la soucoupe
S el platillo
G die Untertasse

**teaspoon**
F la petite cuillère
S la cucharadita
G der Teelöffel

**table cloth**
F la nappe
S el mantel
G die Tischdecke

**napkin**
F la serviette de table
S la servilleta
G die Serviette

**table**
F la table
S la mesa
G der Tisch

**chairs**
F les chaises
S las sillas
G die Stühle

**fork**
F la fourchette
S el tenedor
G die Gabel

**spoon**
F la cuillère
S la cuchara
G der Löffel

**salt**
F le sel
S la sal
G das Salz

**pepper**
F le poivre
S la pimienta
G der Pfeffer

**knife**
F le couteau
S el cuchillo
G das Messer

**jug**
F le pot à eau
S la jarra
G die Kanne

**fruit**
F le fruit / les fruits
S la fruta
G das Obst

**glass**
F le verre
S la copa
G das Glas

**bottle**
F la bouteille
S la botella
G die Flasche

# The Playroom
## La salle de jeux

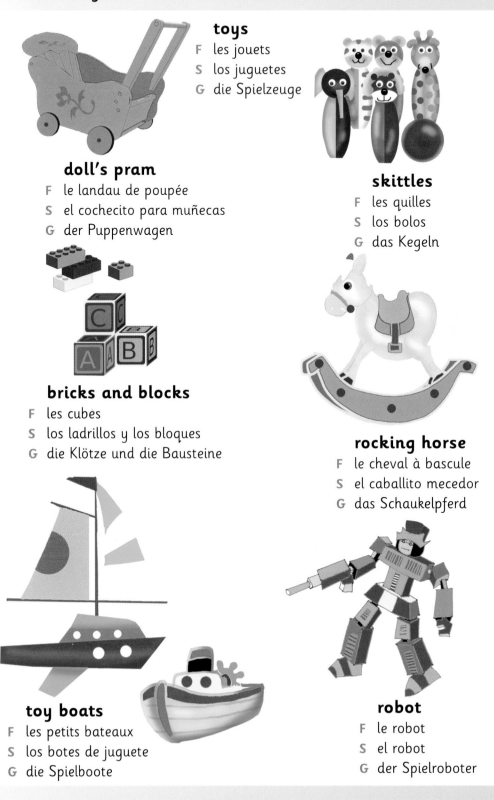

**toys**
F les jouets
S los juguetes
G die Spielzeuge

**doll's pram**
F le landau de poupée
S el cochecito para muñecas
G der Puppenwagen

**skittles**
F les quilles
S los bolos
G das Kegeln

**bricks and blocks**
F les cubes
S los ladrillos y los bloques
G die Klötze und die Bausteine

**rocking horse**
F le cheval à bascule
S el caballito mecedor
G das Schaukelpferd

**toy boats**
F les petits bateaux
S los botes de juguete
G die Spielboote

**robot**
F le robot
S el robot
G der Spielroboter

### doll's house
F  la maison de poupée
S  la casita de muñecas
G  das Puppenhaus

### skateboard
F  le skateboard
S  la tabla de skate
G  das Skateboard

### soft toys
F  les peluches
S  los peluches
G  die Plüschtiere

### teddy
F  l'ours en peluche
S  el osito
G  der Teddybär

### castle
F  le château
S  el castillo
G  das Schloss

### toy train set
F  le train
S  el juego de trenes
G  die Spielzeugeisenbahn

### toy cars
F  les petites voitures
S  los autos de juguete
G  die Spielautos

# Things in the House
## À la maison

### rug
F  le tapis
S  la alfombra
G  der Vorleger

### laptop
F  l'ordinateur portable
S  la computadora portátil
G  der Laptop

### stool
F  le tabouret
S  el banco
G  der Stuhl

### table lamp
F  la lampe
S  la lámpara de mesa
G  die Tischlampe

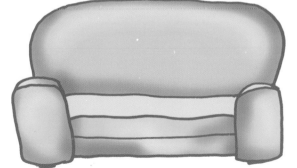

### settee
F  le canapé
S  el sillón
G  das Sofa

### bookcase
**F** la bibliothèque / l'étagère
**S** la estantería para libros
**G** der Bücherschrank

### sideboard
**F** le buffet
**S** el aparador
**G** die Anrichte

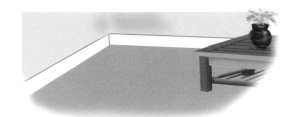

### dressing table
**F** la coiffeuse
**S** el tocador
**G** der Schminktisch

### carpet
**F** le tapis
**S** la alfombra
**G** der Teppich

### coffee table
**F** la table basse
**S** la mesa de centro
**G** der Kaffeetisch

# The Garden
Le jardin

**barbecue**

F le barbecue
S la barbacoa
G der Grill

**garden tools**

F les outils de jardinage
S las herramientas de jardín
G die Gartengeräte

**wheelbarrow**

F la brouette
S la carretilla
G die Schubkarre

**shed**

F la remise / le cabanon
S el cobertizo
G der Schuppen

**lawnmower**

F la tondeuse à gazon
S el cortacésped
G der Rasenmäher

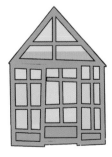

**pond**

F l'etang / la mare
S el estanque
G der Teich

**greenhouse**

F la serre
S el vivero
G das Treibhaus

# The House
## La maison

### door
F  la porte
S  la puerta
G  die Tür

### window
F  la fenêtre
S  la ventana
G  das Fenster

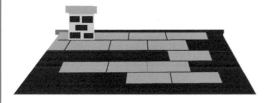

### chimney
F  la cheminée
S  la chimenea
G  der Schornstein

### roof
F  le toit
S  el techo
G  das Dach

### garage
F  le garage
S  el garaje
G  die Garage

### fence
F  la clôture
S  el cerco
G  der Zaun

### wall
F  le mur
S  la pared
G  die Mauer

# In the Workshop
## Dans l'atelier

### paint brushes

F les pinceaux
S los pinceles
G die Pinsel

### paint pots

F les pots de peinture
S los tarros de pintura
G die Farbtöpfe

### car battery

F la batterie de voiture
S la batería del auto
G die Autobatterie

### screws

F les vis
S los tornillos
G die Schrauben

### nails

F les clous
S los clavos
G die Nägel

### saw

F la scie
S la sierra
G die Säge

### spanners

F les clés
S las llaves de tuercas
G der Schraubenschlüssel

### drill
F la perceuse
S el taladro
G der Bohrer

### screwdriver
F le tournevis
S el destornillador
G der Schrauber

### hammer
F le marteau
S el martillo
G der Hammer

### tape measure
F le mètre
S la cinta métrica
G das Metermaß

### axe
F la hache
S el hacha
G die Axt

### bucket
F le seau
S el balde
G der Eimer

### toolbox
F la boîte à outils
S la valija de herramientas
G der Werkzeugkasten

31

# Pets
## Les animaux domestiques

### cat
- F le chat
- S el gato
- G die Katze

### kitten
- F le chaton
- S el gatito
- G das Kätzchen

### mouse
- F la souris
- S el ratón
- G die Maus

### guinea pig
- F le cochon d'inde
- S el conejillo de Indias
- G das Meerschweinchen

### parrot
- F le perroquet
- S el loro
- G die Papagei

### hamster
- F le hamster
- S el hámster
- G der Hamster

### budgerigar
- F la perruche
- S el periquito
- G der Wellensittich

### horse
- F le cheval
- S el caballo
- G das Pferd

### donkey
- F l'âne
- S el burro
- G der Esel

### rabbit

F le lapin
S el conejo
G das Kaninchen

### cockatoo

F le cacatoès
S la cacatúa
G der Kakadu

### gerbil

F la gerbille
S el gerbo
G die Wüstenrennmaus

### puppy

F le chiot
S el cachorro
G der Welpe

### dog

F le chien
S el perro
G der Hund

### fish

F le poisson
S el pez
G der Fisch

# Out in the Street
## Dans la rue

**bicycle**
F le vélo
S la bicicleta
G das Fahrrad

**lamppost**
F le réverbère
S el farol
G der Laternenpfahl

**traffic lights**
F les feux de circulation
S el semáforo
G die Ampel

**car**
F la voiture
S el auto
G das Auto

**bus stop**
F l'arrêt de bus
S la parada de autobús
G die Bushaltestelle

### truck
F le camion
S el camión
G der Lastwagen

### bus
F le bus
S el autobús
G der Bus

### police car
F la voiture de police
S la patrulla
G das Polizeiauto

### motorcycle
F la moto
S la motocicleta
G das Motorrad

### taxi
F le taxi
S el taxi
G das Taxi

### lorry
F le camion
S el camión
g der Transporter

# In the Town
## En ville

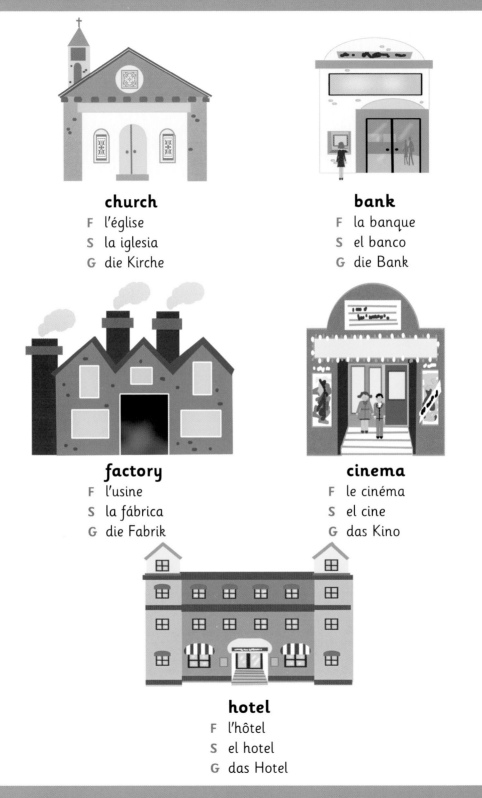

**church**
F l'église
S la iglesia
G die Kirche

**bank**
F la banque
S el banco
G die Bank

**factory**
F l'usine
S la fábrica
G die Fabrik

**cinema**
F le cinéma
S el cine
G das Kino

**hotel**
F l'hôtel
S el hotel
G das Hotel

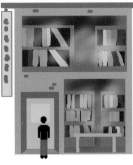

### library
F la bibliothèque
S la biblioteca
G die Bibliothek

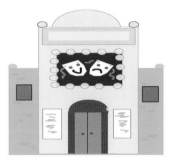

### theatre
F le théâtre
S el teatro
G das Theater

### stadium
F le stade
S el estadio
G das Stadion

### office block
F les bureaux
S el edificio de oficinas
G der Büroblock

### skyscraper
F le gratte-ciel
S el rascacielos
G der Wolkenkratzer

# In the Supermarket
## Au supermarché

### checkout
- F  la caisse
- S  la caja
- G  die Kasse

### vegetables
- F  les légumes
- S  la verdura
- G  das Gemüse

### credit card
- F  la carte de crédit
- S  la tarjeta de crédito
- G  die Kreditkarte

### money
- F  l'argent
- S  el dinero
- G  das Geld

### purse
- F  le porte-monnaie
- S  el monedero
- G  das Portemonnaie

### milk
F le lait
S la leche
G die Milch

### fish
F le poisson
S el pescado
G der Fisch

### basket
F le panier
S el canasto
G der Einkaufskorb

### cheese
F le fromage
S el queso
G der Käse

### bag
F le sac
S la bolsa
G die Tasche

### cereal
F les céréales
S el cereal
G die Cornflakes

### trolley
F le chariot
S el carrito
G der Einkaufswagen

### turkey
F la dinde
S el pavo
G der Truthahn

# Fruit
## Les fruits

### orange
F l'orange
S la naranja
G die Orange

### grapes
F les raisins
S las uvas
G die Weintrauben

### banana
F la banane
S la banana
G die Banane

### lemon
F le citron
S el limón
G die Zitrone

### cherries
F les cerises
S las cerezas
G die Kirschen

### pineapple
F l'ananas
S la piña
G die Ananas

### apple
F la pomme
S la manzana
G der Apfel

### grapefruit
F le pamplemousse
S el pomelo
G die Grapefruit

### pear
F la poire
S la pera
G die Birne

### plums
F les prunes
S las ciruelas
G die Pflaumen

### melon
F le melon
S el melón
G die Melone

### strawberries
F les fraises
S las fresas
G die Erdbeeren

# Vegetables
## Les légumes

# Las hortalizas
## Das Gemüse

**potatoes**
F les pommes de terre
S las patatas
G die Kartoffeln

**carrots**
F les carottes
S las zanahorias
G die Karotten

**tomatoes**
F les tomates
S los tomates
G die Tomaten

**cabbage**
F le chou
S el repollo
G der Kohl

**cucumber**
F le concombre
S el pepino
G die Gurke

**mushrooms**
F les champignons
S los hongos
G die Pilze

**onions**
F les oignons
S las cebollas
G die Zwiebeln

**lettuce**
F la laitue
S la lechuga
G der Salat

**peas**
F les petits pois
S las arvejas
G die Erbsen

**pumpkin**
F la citrouille
S la calabaza
G der Kürbis

**green beans**
F les haricots verts
S los frijoles verdes
G die Brechbohnen

**corn on the cob**
F les épis de maïs
S el maiz en la mazorca
G die Maiskolben

# More Things to Eat and Drink
## Plus de choses à boire et à manger

**nuts**
F les noix
S las nueces
G die Nüsse

**honey**
F le miel
S la miel
G der Honig

**chocolate**
F le chocolat
S el chocolate
G die Schokolade

**soup**
F la soupe
S la sopa
G die Suppe

**pizza**
F la pizza
S la pizza
G die Pizza

**eggs**
F les œufs
S los huevos
G die Eier

**cakes**
F les gâteaux
S las tortas
G die Kuchen

### fries
F les frites
S las patatas fritas
G die Pommes

### salad
F la salade
S la ensalada
G der Salat

### bread
F le pain
S el pan
G das Brot

### toast
F la tartine grillée
S las tostadas
G der Toast

### sandwich
F le sandwich
S el emparedado
G das Sandwich

### hot dog
F le hot-dog
S el perro caliente
G der Hot Dog

### spaghetti
F les spaghettis
S los espaguetis
G die Spaghetti

### pie
F la tourte
S el pastel
G die Pastete

# Fun in the Park

S'amuser au parc

### sandpit
F  le bac à sable
S  el arenero
G  der Sandkasten

### bench
F  le banc
S  el banco
G  die Bank

### roundabout
F  le manège
S  el carrusel
G  das Karussell

### climbing frame
F  la cage à poules
S  la trepadora
G  das Klettergerüst

### skateboard
F  le skateboard
S  la tabla de skate
G  das Skateboard

### scooter
F  la trotinette
S  el patinete
G  der Roller

### slide
F  le toboggan
S  el tobogán
G  die Rutsche

### seesaw
F  la balançoire
S  el sube y baja
G  die Wippe

### kite
F  le cerf-volant
S  el barrilete
G  der Drachen

### ball
F  le ballon
S  la pelota
G  der Ball

# People at Work
## Les métiers

**shopkeeper**
F la marchande
S la tendera
G die Ladenbesitzerin

**traffic warden**
F l'agent de circulation
S la policía de tránsito
G die Polizeihelferin

**librarian**
F la bibliothécaire
S la bibliotecaria
G die Bibliothekarin

**scientist**
F le scientifique
S el científico
G der Wissenschaftler

**electrician**
F l'électricien
S el electricista
G der Elektriker

**hairdresser**
F le coiffeur
S la peluquera
G die Frisörin

**judge**
F le juge
S el juez
G der Richter

**singer**
F la chanteuse
S la cantante
G die Sängerin

**miner**
F le mineur
S el minero
G der Bergmann

**dancer**
F la danseuse
S la bailarina
G die Tänzerin

**baker**
F le boulanger
S el panadero
G der Bäcker

**policeman**
F le policier
S el policía
G der Polizist

# More People at Work
## Plus de métiers

### decorator
F le peintre
S el decorador
G der Dekorateur

### nurse
F l'infirmière
S la enfermera
G die Krankenschwester

### musician
F la musicienne
S la música
G die Musikerin

### gardener
F le jardinier
S el jardinero
G der Gärtner

### actor
F l'acteur
S el actor
G der Schauspieler

### secretary
F la secrétaire
S la secretaria
G die Sekretärin

### fireman
F le pompier
S el bombero
G der Feuerwehrmann

### carpenter
F le charpentier
S el carpintero
G der Tischler

### mechanic
**F** le mécanicien
**S** el mecánico
**G** der Mechaniker

### removal man
**F** le déménageur
**S** el personal de mudanzas
**G** der Möbelpacker

### astronaut
**F** l'astronaute
**S** el astronauta
**G** der Astronaut

### postman
**F** le facteur
**S** el cartero
**G** der Briefträger

### builder
**F** le maçon
**S** el albañil
**G** der Baumeister

### butcher
**F** le boucher
**S** el carnicero
**G** der Fleischer

### farmer
**F** l'agriculteur
**S** el granjero
**G** der Bauer

### vet
**F** le vétérinaire
**S** el veterinario
**G** der Tierarzt

# In the Office
## Au bureau

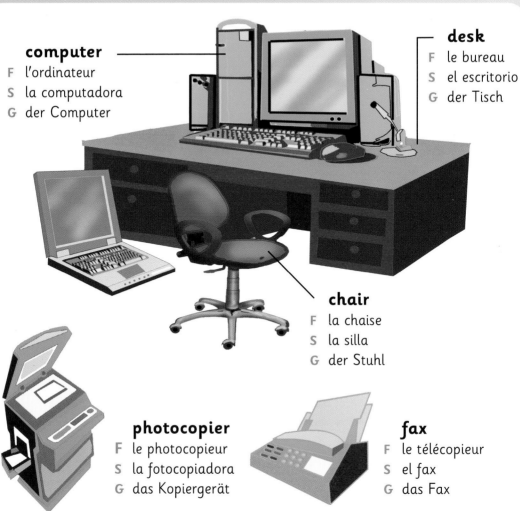

**computer**
F l'ordinateur
S la computadora
G der Computer

**desk**
F le bureau
S el escritorio
G der Tisch

**chair**
F la chaise
S la silla
G der Stuhl

**photocopier**
F le photocopieur
S la fotocopiadora
G das Kopiergerät

**fax**
F le télécopieur
S el fax
G das Fax

**filing cabinet**
F le classeur
S el archivador
G der Aktenschrank

**wastepaper bin**
F la corbeille à papier
S la papelera
G der Papierkorb

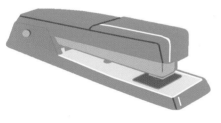

### stapler
F l'agrafeuse
S la grapadora
G der Hefter

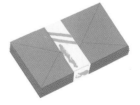

### envelopes
F les enveloppes
S los sobres
G die Briefumschläge

### rubber
F la gomme
S la goma
G der Radiergummi

### ruler
F la règle
S la regla
G das Lineal

### calculator
F la calculatrice
S la calculadora
G der Rechner

### calendar
F le calendrier
S el calendario
G der Kalender

### paper
F le papier
S el papel
G das Papier

### pen
F le stylo
S el bolígrafo
G der Kuli

### pencil
F le crayon
S el lápiz
G der Bleistift

# At the Garage
## Au garage

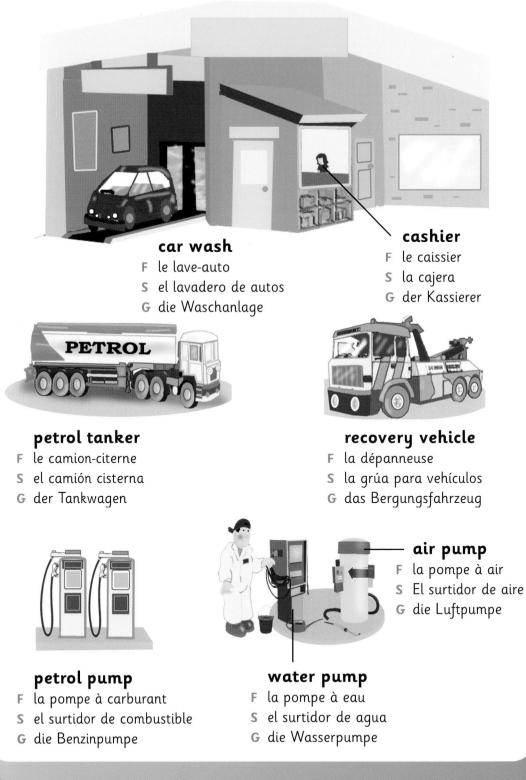

**car wash**
F le lave-auto
S el lavadero de autos
G die Waschanlage

**cashier**
F le caissier
S la cajera
G der Kassierer

**petrol tanker**
F le camion-citerne
S el camión cisterna
G der Tankwagen

**recovery vehicle**
F la dépanneuse
S la grúa para vehículos
G das Bergungsfahrzeug

**air pump**
F la pompe à air
S El surtidor de aire
G die Luftpumpe

**petrol pump**
F la pompe à carburant
S el surtidor de combustible
G die Benzinpumpe

**water pump**
F la pompe à eau
S el surtidor de agua
G die Wasserpumpe

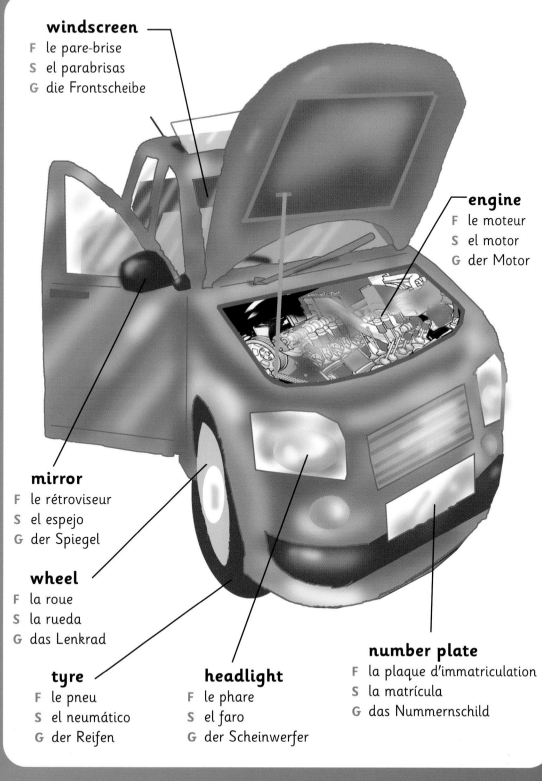

**windscreen**
F le pare-brise
S el parabrisas
G die Frontscheibe

**engine**
F le moteur
S el motor
G der Motor

**mirror**
F le rétroviseur
S el espejo
G der Spiegel

**wheel**
F la roue
S la rueda
G das Lenkrad

**tyre**
F le pneu
S el neumático
G der Reifen

**headlight**
F le phare
S el faro
G der Scheinwerfer

**number plate**
F la plaque d'immatriculation
S la matrícula
G das Nummernschild

# At the Doctor
## Chez le docteur

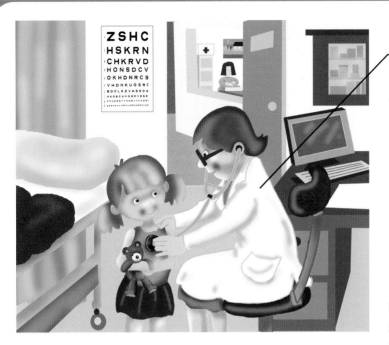

**doctor**
F  la médecin
S  el doctor
G  die Ärztin

**medicine**
F  le médicament
S  el remedio
G  das Medikament

**stethoscope**
F  le stéthoscope
S  el estetoscopio
G  das Stethoskop

**pills**
F  les médicaments
S  las pastillas
G  die Tabletten

**torch**
F  la torche
S  la linterna
G  die Taschenlampe

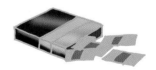

**thermometer**
F  le thermomètre
S  el termómetro
G  das Fieberthermometer

**bandage**
F  le pansement
S  la venda
G  der Verband

**plasters**
F  le pansement
S  las curitas
G  die Pflaster

# At the Dentist
## Chez la dentiste

# En el dentista
## Beim Zahnarzt

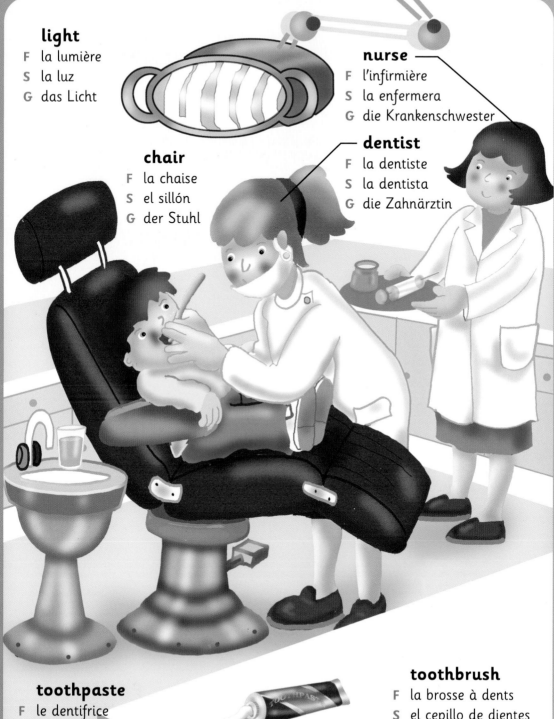

**light**
F la lumière
S la luz
G das Licht

**nurse**
F l'infirmière
S la enfermera
G die Krankenschwester

**chair**
F la chaise
S el sillón
G der Stuhl

**dentist**
F la dentiste
S la dentista
G die Zahnärztin

**toothpaste**
F le dentifrice
S la pasta de dientes
G die Zahnpasta

**toothbrush**
F la brosse à dents
S el cepillo de dientes
G die Zahnbürste

# In Hospital
## À l'hôpital

### crutches
F les béquilles
S las muletas
G die Krücke

### wheelchair
F le fauteuil roulant
S la silla de ruedas
G der Rollstuhl

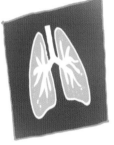

### x-ray
F la radiographie
S los rayos X
G das Röntgenbild

### plaster
F le plâtre
S el yeso
G der Gips

### pill
F le médicament
S la pastilla
G die Tablette

### fruit
F les fruits
S la fruta
G das Obst

### tools
F les outils
S los instrumentos
G die Werkzeuge

### thermometer
F le thermomètre
S el termómetro
G das Thermometer

# Games & Pastimes
## Les jeux et les loisirs

 **fun with paper**
F découper et coller
S jugar con papel
G Spaß mit Papier

 **dancing**
F danser
S bailar
G das Tanzen

 **listening to music**
F écouter de la musique
S escuchar música
G die Musik hören

 **sewing**
F coudre
S coser
G das Nähen

 **cooking**
F faire la cuisine
S cocinar
G das Kochen

 **reading**
F lire
S leer
G das Lesen

 **walking**
F se promener
S caminar
G das Spazierengehen

 **singing**
F chanter
S cantar
G das Singen

### writing
F écrire
S escribir
G das Schreiben

### playing cards
F les cartes à jouer
S jugar a las cartas
G das Kartenspielen

### dressing up
F se déguiser
S disfrazarse
G das Verkleiden

### computer games
F le jeu sur ordinateur
S juegos de computadora
G das Computerspiel

### board games
F les jeux de société
S juegos de caja
G die Brettspiele

# Sports
## Les sports

**horse riding**
F l'équitation
S montar a caballo
G das Pferdereiten

**tennis**
F le tennis
S tenis
G das Tennis

**swimming**
F la natation
S nadar
G das Schwimmen

**cycling**
F le cyclisme
S pasear en bicicleta
G das Radfahren

**ice skating**
F le patinage
S patinar sobre hielo
G das Eislaufen

**cricket**
F le cricket
S cricket
G das Kricket

**basketball**
F le basket-ball
S básquetbol
G der Basketball

### baseball
F le base-ball
S baseball
G der Baseball

### rugby
F le rugby
S rugby
G das Rugby

### football
F le foot(ball)
S fútbol
G der Fußball

### golf
F le golf
S golf
G das Golf

### badminton
F le badminton
S badminton
G das Badminton

### gymnastics
F la gymnastique
S gimnasia
G die Gymnastik

### running
F la course
S correr
G das Laufen

# On the Farm
## À la ferme

### farmer
F l'agriculteur
S el granjero
G der Bauer

### apple trees
F les pommiers
S los manzanos
G der Apfelbaum

### cockerel
F le coq
S el gallito
G das Hähnchen

### tractor
F le tracteur
S el tractor
G der Traktor

### bull
F le taureau
S el toro
G der Stier

### duck
F le canard
S el pato
G die Ente

### ducklings
F les canetons
S el patito
G die Entchen

### chicks
F les poussins
S los pollitos
G die Küken

### hen
F la poule
S la gallina
G das Huhn

**cow**
F la vache
S la vaca
G die Kuh

**calf**
F le veau
S el ternero
G das Kalb

**sheep**
F le mouton
S la oveja
G das Schaf

**lamb**
F l'agneau
S el cordero
G das Lamm

**goose**
F l'oie
S el ganso
G die Gans

**goslings**
F les oisons
S el gansito
G die Gänschen

**piglet**
F le porcelet
S el cochinillo
G das Schweinchen

**pig**
F le cochon
S el cerdo
G das Schwein

**goat**
F la chèvre
S la cabra
G die Ziege

**kid**
F le chevreau
S el cabrito
G das Kind

**horse**
F le cheval
S el caballo
G das Pferd

**foal**
F le poulain
S el potro
G das Fohlen

**turkey**
F la dinde
S el pavo
G der Truthahn

**haystack**
F les bottes de paille
S el montón de heno
G der Heuhaufen

# At School
## À l'école

### globe
F le globe
S el globo terráqueo
G der Globus

### lunch box
F le pique-nique
S el portaviandas
G die Brotdose

### exercise books
F les cahiers
S los libros de ejercicios
G die Arbeitsbücher

**ABCDEFGHI
JKLMNOPQR
STUVWXYZ
1234567890**

### alphabet
F l'alphabet
S el alfabeto
G das Alphabet

Aa

### teacher
F la maîtresse
S la maestra
G die Lehrerin

### whiteboard
F le tableau blanc
S la pizarra
G die Weißwandtafel

### notebook
F le bloc-notes
S el cuaderno
G das Notizbuch

### wall chart
F le tableau mural
S el mural
G die Wandkarte

### backpack
F le sac à dos
S la mochila
G der Rucksack

### drawing
F le dessin
S el dibujo
G die Zeichnung

### pencil case
F la trousse
S el portalápices
G die Federmappe

### pupils
F les élèves
S los alumnos
G die Schüler

# Going Places: By Train
## Voyager: en train

### railway station
F la gare
S la estación de tren
G der Bahnhof

### platform
F le quai
S la plataforma
G das Gleis

### diesel engine
F la locomotive diesel
S el motor Diesel
G der Dieselmotor

### buffet car
F le wagon-restaurant
S el vagón-restaurante
G der Bistrowagen

### ticket office
F  le guichet
S  la boletería
G  der Fahrkartenschalter

### luggage
F  les bagages
S  el equipaje
G  das Gepäck

### passenger
F  le passager
S  el pasajero
G  der Passagier

### ticket collector
F  le contrôleur de billets
S  el inspector de boletos
G  der Schaffner

### escalator
F  l'escalier roulant
S  la escalera mecánica
G  der Aufzug

### steam engine
F  la locomotive à vapeur
S  el motor a vapor
G  der Dampfmotor

# Going Places: By Water
## Voyager: sur l'eau

### boat
F le bateau
S el bote
G das Schiff

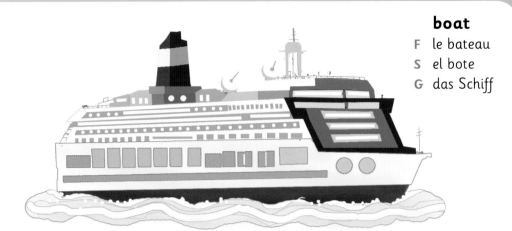

### yacht
F le yacht
S el velero
G die Jacht

### submarine
F le sous-marin
S el submarino
G das U-Boot

### hydrofoil
F l'hydroptère
S el hidroala
G das Tragflächenboot

### anchor
F l'ancre
S el ancla
G der Anker

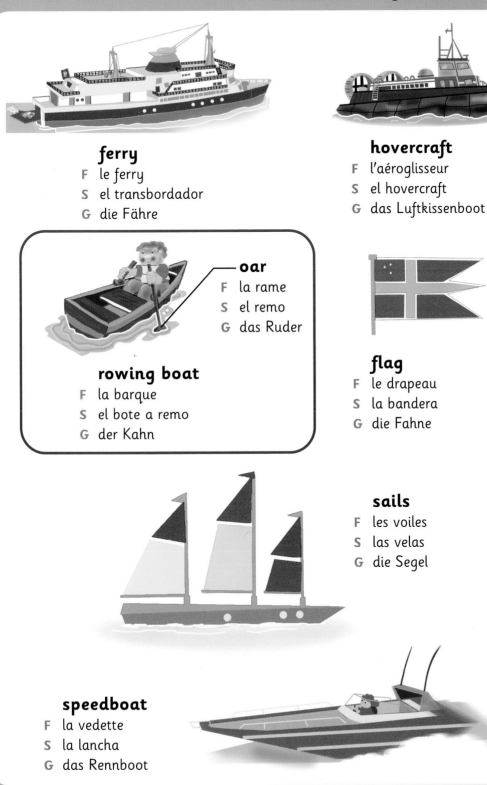

### ferry
F le ferry
S el transbordador
G die Fähre

### hovercraft
F l'aéroglisseur
S el hovercraft
G das Luftkissenboot

### oar
F la rame
S el remo
G das Ruder

### rowing boat
F la barque
S el bote a remo
G der Kahn

### flag
F le drapeau
S la bandera
G die Fahne

### sails
F les voiles
S las velas
G die Segel

### speedboat
F la vedette
S la lancha
G das Rennboot

# Going Places: By Plane
## Voyager: en avion

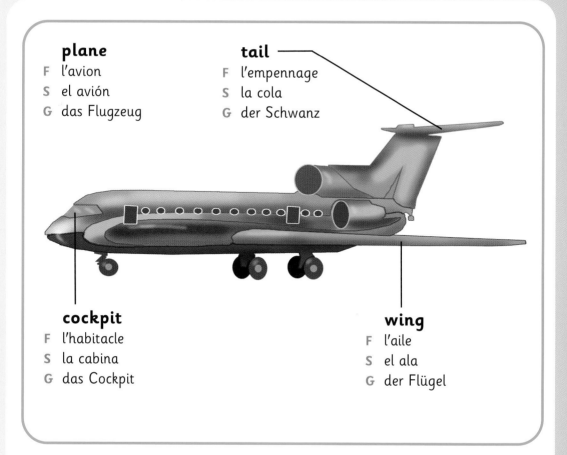

**plane**
F  l'avion
S  el avión
G  das Flugzeug

**tail**
F  l'empennage
S  la cola
G  der Schwanz

**cockpit**
F  l'habitacle
S  la cabina
G  das Cockpit

**wing**
F  l'aile
S  el ala
G  der Flügel

**helicopter**
F  l'hélicoptère
S  el helicóptero
G  der Hubschrauber

**passenger jet**
F  l'avion de ligne
S  el avión de pasajeros
G  das Passagierdüsenflugzeug

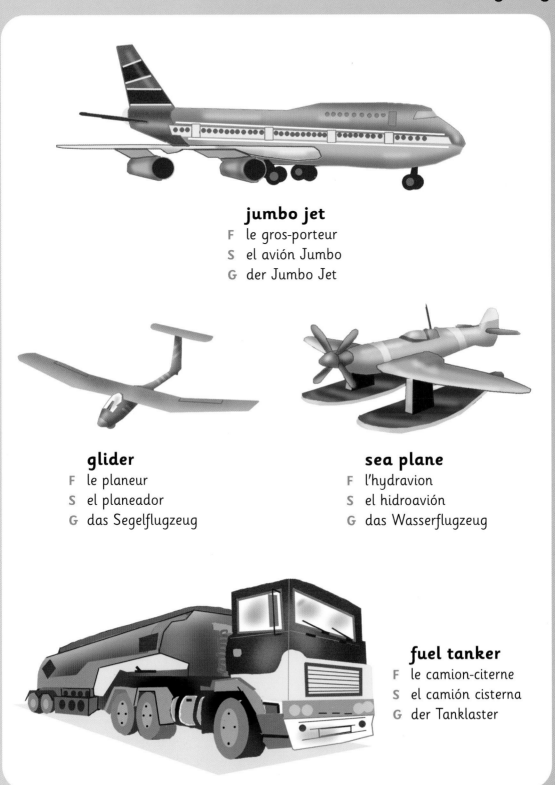

**jumbo jet**

F  le gros-porteur
S  el avión Jumbo
G  der Jumbo Jet

**glider**

F  le planeur
S  el planeador
G  das Segelflugzeug

**sea plane**

F  l'hydravion
S  el hidroavión
G  das Wasserflugzeug

**fuel tanker**

F  le camion-citerne
S  el camión cisterna
G  der Tanklaster

# In the Country
## À la campagne

### balloon
F la montgolfière
S el globo
G der Ballon

### mountain
F la montagne
S la montaña
G der Berg

### trees
F les arbres
S los árboles
G die Bäume

### butterfly
F le papillon
S la mariposa
G der Schmetterling

### rabbit
F le lapin
S el conejo
G das Kaninchen

### hedgehog
F l'hérisson
S el erizo
G der Igel

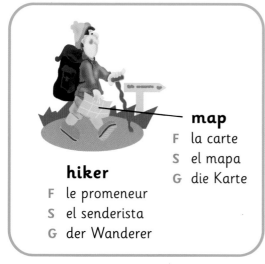

**map**
F la carte
S el mapa
G die Karte

**hiker**
F le promeneur
S el senderista
G der Wanderer

**tent**
F la tente
S la carpa
G das Zelt

**caravan**
F la caravane
S la caravana
G der Wohnwagen

**scarecrow**
F l'épouvantail
S el espantapájaros
G die Vogelscheuche

**fisherman**
F le pêcheur
S el pescador
G der Fischer

**village**
F le village
S el pueblo
G das Dorf

73

# Builders and Buildings
## Les maçons et les bâtiments

### mosque
- F la mosquée
- S la mezquita
- G die Moschee

### cottage
- F le cottage
- S la casa de campo
- G das Landhaus

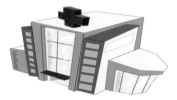

### hospital
- F l'hôpital
- S el hospital
- G das Krankenhaus

### terraced houses
- F les maisons mitoyennes
- S la casas adosadas
- G die Reihenhäuser

### stately home
- F le manoir
- S la mansión
- G der Herrensitz

### fire station
- F la caserne de pompiers
- S la estación de bomberos
- G die Feuerwache

### castle
- F le château
- S el castillo
- G das Schloss

### hard hat
**F** le casque de sécurité
**S** el casco
**G** der Schutzhelm

### brick
**F** la brique
**S** el ladrillo
**G** der Backstein

### trowel
**F** la truelle
**S** la paleta
**G** die Maurerkelle

### bulldozer
**F** le bulldozer
**S** la excavadora
**G** der Bulldozer

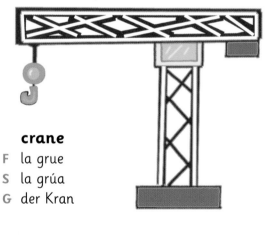

### crane
**F** la grue
**S** la grúa
**G** der Kran

### wheelbarrow
**F** la brouette
**S** la carretilla
**G** die Schubkarre

### plans
**F** les plans
**S** los planos
**G** die Pläne

### plank of wood
**F** la planche
**S** la tabla de madera
**G** das Holzbrett

# Seasons and Weather
## Les saisons et la météo

### spring
- **F** le printemps
- **S** la primavera
- **G** der Frühling

### summer
- **F** l'été
- **S** el verano
- **G** der Sommer

### sunshine
- **F** le soleil
- **S** soleado
- **G** der Sonnenschein

### rain
- **F** la pluie
- **S** la lluvia
- **G** der Regen

### storm
- **F** la tempête
- **S** la tormenta
- **G** das Gewitter

### lightning
- **F** la foudre
- **S** el rayo
- **G** der Blitz

### rainbow
- **F** l'arc-en-ciel
- **S** el arcoiris
- **G** der Regenbogen

### autumn

F l'automne
S el otoño
G der Herbst

### winter

F l'hiver
S el invierno
G der Winter

### wind

F le vent
S el viento
G der Wind

### ice

F la glace
S el hielo
G das Eis

### snow

F la neige
S la nieve
G der Schnee

# Wild Animals
## Les animaux sauvages

**tiger**
- F le tigre
- S el tigre
- G der Tiger

**elephant**
- F l'éléphant
- S el elefante
- G der Elefant

**rhino**
- F le rhinocéros
- S el rinoceronte
- G das Nashorn

**lion**
- F le lion
- S el león
- G der Löwe

**zebra**
- F le zèbre
- S la cebra
- G das Zebra

**panda**
- F le panda
- S el panda
- G der Panda

**hippo**
- F l'hippopotame
- S el hipopótamo
- G das Nilpferd

**crocodile**
- F le crocodile
- S el cocodrilo
- G das Krokodil

**monkey**
- F le singe
- S el mono
- G der Affe

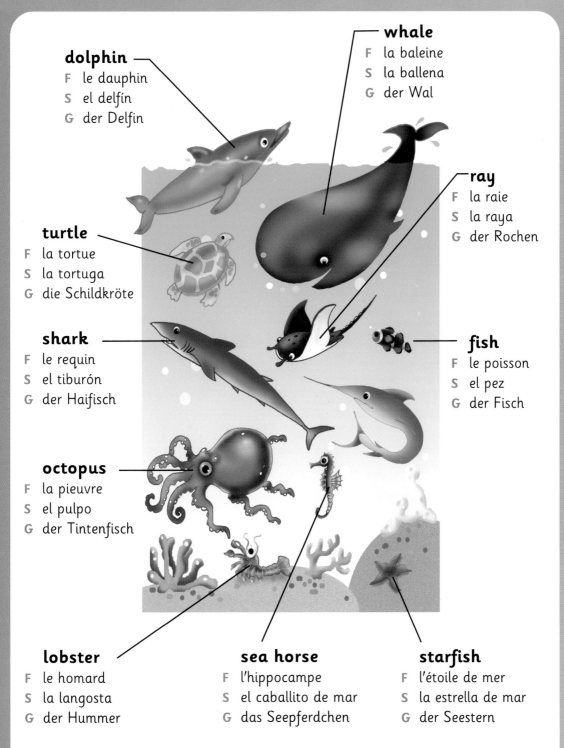

**dolphin**
F le dauphin
S el delfín
G der Delfin

**whale**
F la baleine
S la ballena
G der Wal

**ray**
F la raie
S la raya
G der Rochen

**turtle**
F la tortue
S la tortuga
G die Schildkröte

**shark**
F le requin
S el tiburón
G der Haifisch

**fish**
F le poisson
S el pez
G der Fisch

**octopus**
F la pieuvre
S el pulpo
G der Tintenfisch

**lobster**
F le homard
S la langosta
G der Hummer

**sea horse**
F l'hippocampe
S el caballito de mar
G das Seepferdchen

**starfish**
F l'étoile de mer
S la estrella de mar
G der Seestern

# More Wild Animals
## Plus d'animaux sauvages

**penguin**
F le pingouin
S el pingüino
G der Pinguin

**walrus**
F le morse
S la morsa
G das Walross

**seal**
F le phoque
S la foca
G der Seehund

**polar bear**
F l'ours polaire
S el oso polar
G der Eisbär

**moose**
F l'élan
S el alce
G der Elch

**koala**
F le koala
S el koala
G der Koala

**swan**
F le cygne
S el cisne
G der Schwan

**woodpecker**
F le pivert
S el pájaro carpintero
G der Specht

**kangaroo**
F le kangourou
S el canguro
G das Känguru

**owl**
F le hibou
S el búho
G die Eule

**leopard**
F le léopard
S el leopardo
G der Leopard

**snakes**
F les serpents
S las víboras
G die Schlangen

**sloth**
F le paresseux
S el perezoso
G das Faultier

**gorilla**
F le gorille
S el gorila
G der Gorilla

**giraffe**
F la girafe
S la jirafa
G die Giraffe

**ostrich**
F l'autruche
S el avestruz
G der Strauß

**stork**
F la cigogne
S la cigüeña
G der Storch

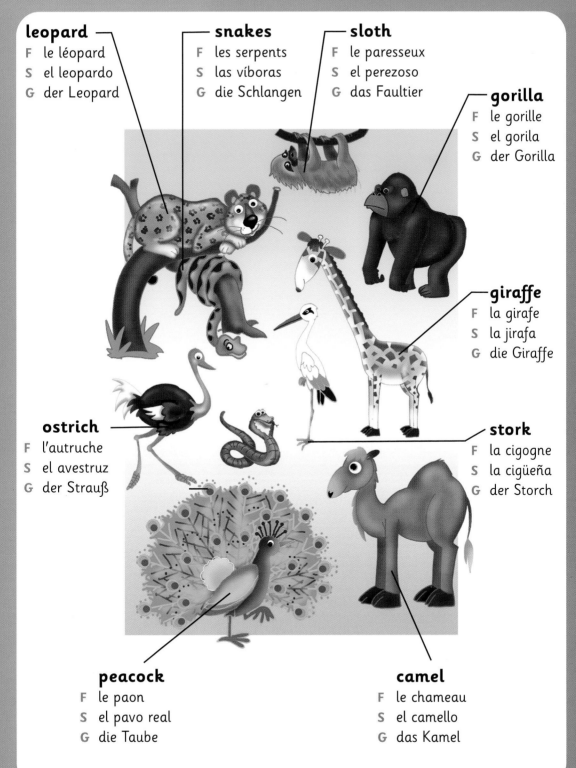

**peacock**
F le paon
S el pavo real
G die Taube

**camel**
F le chameau
S el camello
G das Kamel

# Insects and Creepy-Crawlies

Insectos y rastreros

Les insectes et autres petits animaux Die Insekten und die Krabbeltiere

### centipede
F le mille-pattes
S el ciempiés
G der Tausendfüßer

### praying mantis
F la mante religieuse
S la mantis religiosa
G die Gottesanbeterin

### snail
F l'escargot
S el caracol
G die Schnecke

### ladybird
F la coccinelle
S la mariquita
G der Marienkäfer

### butterfly
F le papillon
S la mariposa
G der Schmetterling

### wasp
F la guêpe
S la avispa
G die Wespe

### caterpillar
F la chenille
S el gusano
G die Raupe

### scorpion
F le scorpion
S el escorpión
G der Skorpion

### slug
F la limace
S la babosa
G die Nacktschnecke

### beetle
F le scarabée
S el escarabajo
G der Käfer

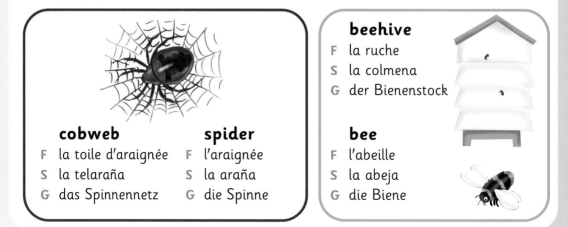

### cobweb
F la toile d'araignée
S la telaraña
G das Spinnennetz

### spider
F l'araignée
S la araña
G die Spinne

### beehive
F la ruche
S la colmena
G der Bienenstock

### bee
F l'abeille
S la abeja
G die Biene

# Animal Parts
## Les membres des animaux

### Partes de animales
### Die Tierteile

**beak**
F le bec
S el pico
G der Schnabel

**hump**
F la bosse
S la joroba
G der Höcker

**wing**
F l'aile
S el ala
G der Flügel

**antlers**
F les bois
S la cornamenta
G das Geweih

**pouch**
F la poche
S la bolsa
G der Beutel

**hoof**
F le sabot
S la pezuña
G der Huf

**trunk**
F la trompe
S la trompa
G der Rüssel

**tusk**
F les défenses
S el colmillo
G der Stoßzahn

**tail**
F la queue
S la cola
G der Schwanz

**shell**
F la coquille
S el caparazón
G das Gehäuse

**paw**
F la patte
S la garra
G die Pfote

# Plants
## Les plantes

### seeds
- **F** les graines
- **S** las semillas
- **G** das Pflanzgut

### indoor plant
- **F** la plante d'appartement
- **S** las plantas interiores
- **G** die Zimmerpflanze

### cactus
- **F** le cactus
- **S** el cactus
- **G** der Kaktus

### bush
- **F** le buisson
- **S** el arbusto
- **G** der Busch

### bulb
- **F** le bulbe
- **S** el bulbo
- **G** die Blumenzwiebel

### bramble
- **F** la ronce
- **S** la zarza
- **G** die Brombeere

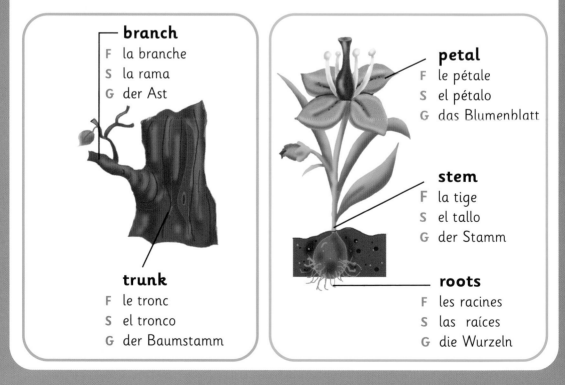

### branch
- **F** la branche
- **S** la rama
- **G** der Ast

### trunk
- **F** le tronc
- **S** el tronco
- **G** der Baumstamm

### petal
- **F** le pétale
- **S** el pétalo
- **G** das Blumenblatt

### stem
- **F** la tige
- **S** el tallo
- **G** der Stamm

### roots
- **F** les racines
- **S** las raíces
- **G** die Wurzeln

# Flowers
## Fleurs

### tulip
F la tulipe
S el tulipán
G die Tulpe

### sunflower
F le tournesol
S el girasol
G die Sonnenblume

### rose
F la rose
S la rosa
G die Rose

### poppy
F le coquelicot
S la amapola
G der Mohn

### bluebell
F la Jacinthe des bois
S el jacinto silvestre
G die Glockenblume

### daffodil
F la jonquille
S el narciso
G die Narzisse

### orchid
F l'orchidée
S la orquídea
G die Orchidee

### wild flowers
F les fleurs sauvages
S las flores silvestres
G die wilden Blumen

### bouquet
F le bouquet
S el ramo
G der Blumenstrauß

# Beside the Sea
## Au bord de la mer

**parasol**
F le parasol
S la sombrilla
G der Sonnenschirm

**donkey**
F l'âne
S el burro
G der Esel

**crab**
F le crabe
S el cangrejo
G die Krabbe

**boat**
F le bateau
S el bote
G das Boot

**ball**
F le ballon
S la pelota
G der Ball

**starfish**
F l'étoile de mer
S la estrella de mar
G der Seestern

**shell**
F le coquillage
S la concha
G die Muschel

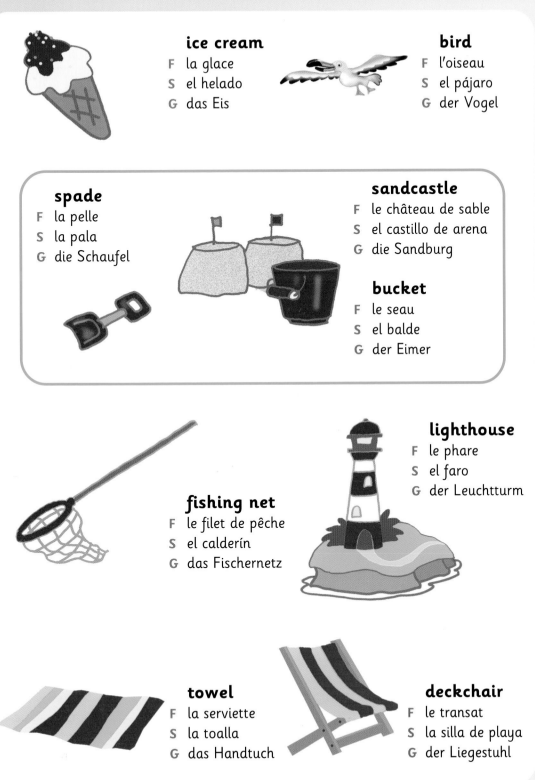

**ice cream**
F  la glace
S  el helado
G  das Eis

**bird**
F  l'oiseau
S  el pájaro
G  der Vogel

**spade**
F  la pelle
S  la pala
G  die Schaufel

**sandcastle**
F  le château de sable
S  el castillo de arena
G  die Sandburg

**bucket**
F  le seau
S  el balde
G  der Eimer

**lighthouse**
F  le phare
S  el faro
G  der Leuchtturm

**fishing net**
F  le filet de pêche
S  el calderín
G  das Fischernetz

**towel**
F  la serviette
S  la toalla
G  das Handtuch

**deckchair**
F  le transat
S  la silla de playa
G  der Liegestuhl

# Having a Party
## Faire une fête

**birthday cake**
F le gâteau d'anniversaire
S la torta de cumpleaños
G die Geburtstagstorte

**present**
F le cadeau
S el regalo
G das Geschenk

**fizzy drink**
F la boisson gazeuse
S la gaseosa
G die Brause

**sweets**
F les bonbons
S los dulces
G die Süßigkeiten

**candle**
F la bougie
S la vela
G die Kerze

### biscuits
F les petits gateaux
S las galletitas
G die Kekse

### jug of orange
F le jus d'orange
S la jarra de jugo de naranja
G die Kanne mit Orangensaft

### camera
F l'appareil photo
S la cámara de fotos
G die Kamera

### birthday card
F la carte d'anniversaire
S la tarjeta de cumpleaños
G die Geburtstagskarte

### paper hat
F le chapeau en papier
S el sombrero de papel
G der Papierhut

### sandwiches
F les sandwiches
S los emparedados
G die Sandwiches

### crisps
F les chips
S las patatas fritas
G die Chips

### balloon
F le ballon
S el globo
G der Luftballon

# Opposites
## Les opposés

### fast
- F  rapide
- S  rápido
- G  schnell

### slow
- F  lent
- S  despacio
- G  langsam

### up
- F  en haut
- S  arriba
- G  hinauf

### down
- F  en bas
- S  abajo
- G  hinunter

### above
- F  au-dessus
- S  encima
- G  oben

### high
- F  haut
- S  alto
- G  hoch

### below
- F  au-dessous
- S  debajo
- G  unten

### wet
- F  mouillé
- S  mojado
- G  feucht

### dry
- F  sec
- S  seco
- G  trocken

### low
- F  bas
- S  bajo
- G  klein

### over
F dessus
S sobre
G über

### behind
F derrière
S detrás
G hinten

### in front
F devant
S delante
G vorne

### under
F dessous
S bajo
G unten

### small
F petit
S pequeño
G klein

### big
F grand
S grande
G groß

### fat
F gros
S gordo
G dick

### thin
F mince
S flaco
G dünn

### out
F dehors
S afuera
G aus

### happy
F joyeux
S feliz
G zufrieden

### sad
F triste
S triste
G traurig

### in
F dedans
S adentro
G in

# Actions
## Les actions

### sitting
- F s'asseoir
- S sentarse
- G das Sitzen

### walking
- F marcher
- S caminar
- G das Spazierengehen

### reading
- F lire
- S leer
- G das Lesen

### drinking
- F boire
- S beber
- G das Trinken

### crying
- F pleurer
- S llorar
- G das Weinen

### kicking
- F donner un coup de pied
- S patear
- G das Kicken

### shouting
- F crier
- S gritar
- G das Schreien

### cutting
- F couper
- S cortar
- G das Schneiden

### writing
- F écrire
- S escribir
- G das Schreiben

### eating
F manger
S comer
G das Essen

### climbing
F monter
S trepar
G das Klettern

### laughing
F rire
S reír
G das Lachen

### jumping
F sauter
S saltar
G das Springen

### hiding
F se cacher
S esconderse
G das Verstecken

### drawing
F dessiner
S dibujar
G das Zeichnen

### running
F courir
S correr
G das Rennen

### cuddling
F câliner
S abrazar
G das Kuscheln

### reaching
F attraper
S agarrar
G das Greifen

### knocking
F frapper
S golpear
G das Klopfen

### playing
F jouer
S jugar
G das Spielen

# Storybook Words
## Les contes

**wizard**

F le sorcier
S el mago
G der Zauberer

**pixie**

F le pixie
S el duendecillo
G der Elf

**prince**

F le prince
S el príncipe
G der Prinz

**princess**

F la princesse
S la princesa
G die Prinzessin

**knight**

F le chevalier
S el caballero
G der Ritter

**dragon**
F le dragon
S el dragón
G der Drache

**giant**
F le géant
S el gigante
G der Gigant

**wolf**
F le loup
S el lobo
G der Wolf

# Colours and Shapes
## Les couleurs et les formes

### a red square
F un carré rouge
S un cuadrado rojo
G rotes Viereck

### a blue cone
F un cône bleu
S un cono azul
G blauer Kegel

### a pink circle
F un cercle rose
S un círculo rosado
G rosa Kreis

### a brown triangle
F un triangle marron
S un triángulo marrón
G braunes Dreieck

### a yellow star
F une étoile jaune
S una estrella amarilla
G gelber Stern

### a black diamond
F un diamant noir
S un diamante negro
G schwarzer Diamant

### a green cube
F un cube vert
S un cubo verde
G grüner Würfel

### a purple crescent
F un croissant violet
S una medialuna violeta
G violetter Halbmond

### an orange curve
F une courbe orange
S un arco naranja
G oranger Bogen

# Numbers
## Les nombres

### one

F un
S uno
G eins

### two

F deux
S dos
G zwei

### three

F trois
S tres
G drei

### four

F quatre
S cuatro
G vier

### five

F cinq
S cinco
G fünf

### six

F six
S seis
G sechs

### seven

F sept
S siete
G sieben

### eight

F huit
S ocho
G acht

### nine

F neuf
S nueve
G neun

### ten

F dix
S diez
G zehn

# Days and Months
## Les jours et les mois

# Los días y los meses
## Die Tage und Monate

**Monday**
F lundi
S lunes
G der Montag

**Tuesday**
F mardi
S martes
G der Dienstag

**Wednesday**
F mercredi
S miércoles
G der Mittwoch

**Thursday**
F jeudi
S jueves
G der Donnerstag

**Friday**
F vendredi
S viernes
G der Freitag

**Saturday**
F samedi
S sábado
G der Samstag

**Sunday**
F dimanche
S domingo
G der Sonntag

**January**
F janvier
S enero
G der Januar

**February**
F février
S febrero
G der Februar

**March**
F mars
S marzo
G der März

**April**
F avril
S abril
G der April

**May**
F mai
S mayo
G der Mai

**June**
F juin
S junio
G der Juni

**July**
F juillet
S julio
G der Juli

**August**
F août
S agosto
G der August

**September**
F septembre
S setiembre
G der September

**October**
F octobre
S octubre
G der Oktober

**November**
F novembre
S noviembre
G der November

**December**
F décembre
S diciembre
G der Dezember

# Special Days
## Les jours de fête

Días especiales<br/>Besondere Tage

### birthday
- F l'anniversaire
- S el cumpleaños
- G der Geburtstag

### holiday
- F les vacances
- S las vacaciones
- G die Ferien

### wedding day
- F le jour du mariage
- S la boda
- G der Hochzeitstag

### Christmas Day
- F le jour de Noël
- S la Navidad
- G der Weihnachtstag

# The Fairground
## La fête foraine

### big wheel
F la grande roue
S la rueda gigante
G das Riesenrad

### hoopla
F le jeu d'anneaux
S el juego de aros
G das Ringwerfen

### ghost train
F le train fantôme
S el tren fantasma
G die Geisterbahn

### roller coaster
**F** les montagnes russes
**S** la montaña rusa
**G** die Achterbahn

### carousel
**F** le manège
**S** el carrusel
**G** das Karussell

### dodgems
**F** les auto-tamponneuses
**S** los autos chocadores
**G** der Autoscooter

### helter skelter
**F** l'Helter Skelter
**S** el tobogán
**G** die spiralförmige Rutsche

# The Circus
## Le cirque

### trapeze artist
F le trapéziste
S el trapecista
G der Trapezkünstler

### unicyclist
F le monocycliste
S el monociclista
G der Einradfahrer

### lion
F le lion
S el león
G der Löwe

### clown
F le clown
S el payaso
G der Clown

## bareback rider

F la cavalière qui monte à cru
S el acróbata a caballo
G der Kunstreiter

## elephant

F l'éléphant
S el elefante
G der Elefant

## acrobat

F l'acrobate
S el acróbata
G der Akrobat

## circus tent

F le chapiteau de cirque
S la carpa del circo
G das Zirkuszelt

## ringmaster

F le Monsieur Loyal
S el entrenador
G der Zirkusdirektor

# The Restaurant
## Le restaurant

### cutlery
F les couverts
S los cubiertos
G das Besteck

### food
F la nourriture
S la comida
G das Essen

### dessert
F le dessert
S el postre
G der Nachtisch

### tray
F le plateau
S la bandeja
G das Tablett

### chef
F le chef cuisinier
S el cocinero
G der Koch

### waiter
F le serveur
S el mesero
G der Kellner

### waitress
F la serveuse
S la camarera
G die Kellnerin

### menu
F le menu
S el menú
G die Speisekarte

### table and chairs
F les tables et les chaises
S las mesa y sillas
G die Tische und die Stühle

# The Cinema
## Le cinéma

**popcorn**
F le pop-corn
S las palomitas de maíz
G das Popcorn

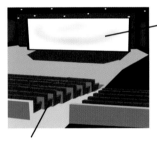

**screen**
F l'écran
S la pantalla
G der Bildschirm

**tickets**
F les billets
S los boletos
G die Karten

**seats**
F les sièges
S los asientos
G die Plätze

**film**
F le film
S la película
G der Film

**torch**
F la torche
S la linterna
G die Tachenlampe

**ice lolly**
F la glace
S el helado de palo
G das Eis am Stiel

**projector**
F l'appareil de projection
S el proyector
G der Beamer

# Fun with Colour
## Jouer avec les couleurs

# Diversión con colores
## Spaß mit Farben

### paint brush
- F le pinceau
- S el pincel
- G der Pinsel

### colouring pencil
- F le crayon de couleur
- S los lápices de colores
- G der Buntstift

### crayon
- F le pastel
- S el lápiz de cera
- G der Wachsmalstift

### yellow
- F jaune
- S amarillo
- G gelb

### red
- F rouge
- S rojo
- G rot

### pink
- F rose
- S rosado
- G rosa

### black
- F noir
- S negro
- G schwarz

### brown
- F marron
- S marrón
- G braun

### white
- F blanc
- S blanco
- G weiß

### blue
- F bleu
- S azul
- G blau

### green
- F vert
- S verde
- G grün

### orange
- F orange
- S naranja
- G orange

### grey
- F gris
- S gris
- G grau

### purple
- F violet
- S violeta
- G violett

### paper
- F le papier
- S el papel
- G das Papier

### paint
- F la peinture
- S la pintura
- G die Farbe

# Fancy Dress
## Le déguisement

# Los disfraces
## Die Verkleidung

### cowboy
F le cow-boy
S el vaquero
G der Cowboy

### american indian
F l'Amérindien
S el indio americano
G der Indianer

### fairy
F la fée
S el hada
G die Fee

### bunny
F le Jeannot lapin
S el conejito
G das Kaninchen

### skeleton
F le squelette
S el esqueleto
G das Skelett

### pirate
F le pirate
S el pirata
G der Pirat

### princess
F la princesse
S la princesa
G die Prinzessin

### witch
F la sorcière
S la bruja
G die Hexe

# Musical Instruments
## Les instruments de musique

# Los instrumentos musicales
## Die Musikinstrumente

**drum**
- F le tambour
- S el tambor
- G die Trommel

**saxophone**
- F le saxophone
- S el saxofón
- G das Saxofon

**xylophone**
- F le xylophone
- S el xilofón
- G das Xylofon

**tambourine**
- F le tambourin
- S la pandereta
- G das Tamburin

**violin**
- F le violon
- S el violín
- G die Geige

**recorder**
- F la flûte à bec
- S la flauta dulce
- G die Blockflöte

**maracas**
- F les maracas
- S las maracas
- G die Rumbakugeln

**bagpipes**
- F la cornemuse
- S la gaita
- G die Sackpfeife

**accordion**
- F l'accordéon
- S el acordeón
- G das Akkordeon

**trumpet**
- F la trompette
- S la trompeta
- G die Trompete

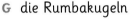

**flute**
- F la flûte
- S la flauta
- G die Flöte

**triangle**
- F le triangle
- S el triángulo
- G der Triangel

**horn**
- F le cor anglais
- S el cuerno
- G das Horn

**harp**
- F la harpe
- S el arpa
- G die Harfe

**cello**
- F le violoncelle
- S el violoncelo
- G das Cello

**piano**
- F le piano
- S el piano
- G das Klavier

# Baby Things
## Pour les bébés

### booties
- **F** les chaussons
- **S** los escarpines
- **G** die Schühchen

### nappy
- **F** la couche
- **S** los pañales
- **G** die Windel

### teddy
- **F** l'ours en peluche
- **S** el osito
- **G** der Teddybär

### bag
- **F** le sac
- **S** el bolso
- **G** die Tasche

### bib
- **F** le bavoir
- **S** el babero
- **G** das Lätzchen

### rattle
- **F** le hochet
- **S** el sonajero
- **G** die Rassel

### bottle
- **F** le biberon
- **S** la mamadera
- **G** die Flasche

### dummy
- **F** la sucette
- **S** el chupete
- **G** der Schnuller

### blanket
- **F** la couverture
- **S** la manta
- **G** die Decke

### baby
- **F** le bébé
- **S** el bebé
- **G** das Baby

### car seat
F le siège auto
S el asiento para auto
G der Kindersitz

### potty
F le pot
S la pelela
G das Töpfchen

### mobile
F le mobile
S el móvil
G das Mobile

### changing mat
F le matelas à langer
S el cambiador
G die Wickeldecke

### playpen
F le parc
S el corralito
G der Laufstall

### cot
F le lit d'enfant
S la cuna
G das Gitterbett

### high chair
F la chaise haute
S la silla alta
G der Hochstuhl

### pram
F le landau
S el cochecito de bebé
G der Kinderwagen

# Senses
## Les sens

**see**

F voir
S ver
G das Sehen

**taste**

F goûter
S saborear
G das Schmecken

**smell**

F sentir
S oler
G das Riechen

**hear**

F entendre
S oír
G das Hören

**touch**

F toucher
S tocar
G das Tasten

# Our Bodies
## Nos corps

Nuestro cuerpo
Unsere Körper

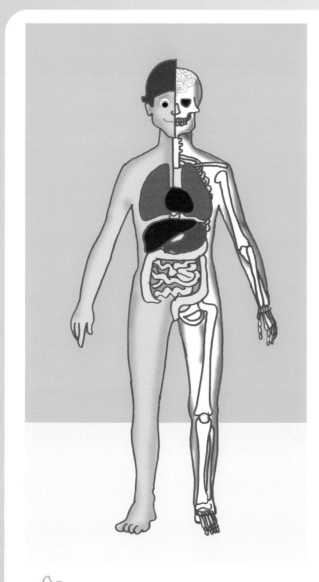

### brain
F le cerveau
S el cerebro
G das Gehirn

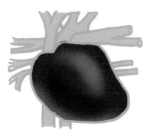

### heart
F le cœur
S el corazón
G das Herz

### bone
F l'os
S el hueso
G der Knochen

### muscle
F le muscle
S el músculo
G der Muskel

# Space
## L'espace

### planet

F la planète
S el planeta
G der Planet

### space shuttle

F la navette spatiale
S la nave espacial
G die Weltraumfähre

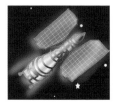

### satellite

F le satellite
S el satélite
G der Satellit

### stars

F les étoiles
S las estrellas
G die Sterne

### moon

F la lune
S la luna
G der Mond

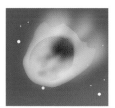

### meteor

F le météore
S el meteoro
G der Meteor

### shooting star

F l'étoile filante
S la estrella fugaz
G die Sternschnuppe

### sun

F le soleil
S el sol
G die Sonne

### Earth

F la Terre
S la tierra
G die Erde

### astronaut

F l'astronaute
S el astronauta
G der Astronaut

# Continents of the World
## Les continents du monde

**North America**
F l'Amérique du Nord
S América del Norte
G Nordamerika

**Arctic Ocean**
F l'océan Arctique
S Océano Ártico
G Arktischer Ozean

**Atlantic Ocean**
F l'océan Atlantique
S Océano Atlántico
G Atlantischer Ozean

**Pacific Ocean**
F l'océan Pacifique
S Océano Pacífico
G Pazifischer Ozean

**South America**
F l'Amérique du Sud
S América del Sur
G Südamerika

**Antarctica**
F l'Antarctique
S Antártida
G Antarktis

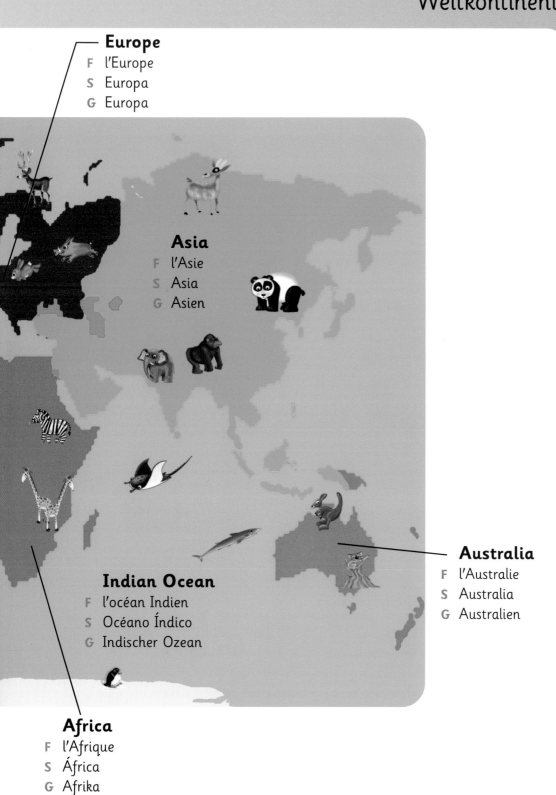

### Europe
F l'Europe
S Europa
G Europa

### Asia
F l'Asie
S Asia
G Asien

### Australia
F l'Australie
S Australia
G Australien

### Indian Ocean
F l'océan Indien
S Océano Índico
G Indischer Ozean

### Africa
F l'Afrique
S África
G Afrika

# Time of Day
## Pendant la journée

Las horas del día
die Tageszeit

### morning
F le matin
S la mañana
G der Morgen

### daytime
F la journée
S el día
G die Tageszeit

### lunchtime
F l'heure du déjeuner
S el mediodía
G die Mittagszeit

### afternoon
F l'après-midi
S la tarde
G der Nachmittag

### evening
F le soir
S el atardecer
G der Abend

### night-time
F la nuit
S la noche
G die Nacht

# Words in this Book

# Words in this Book

# Words in this Book

# Words in this Book

# Words in this Book

# Words in this Book

# Words in this Book

# Words in this Book

# Words in this Book

# Words in this Book